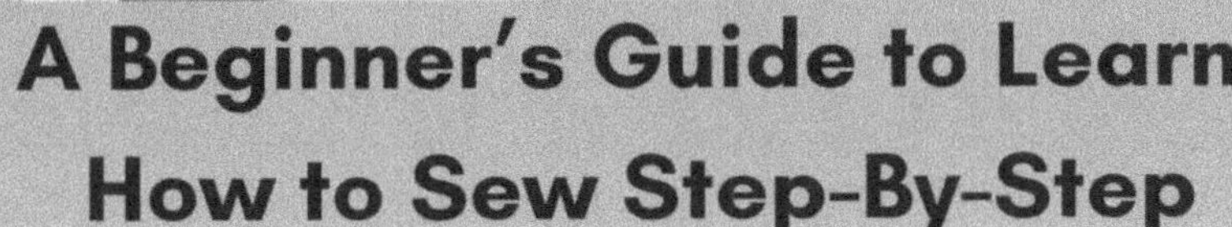

A Beginner's Guide to Learn How to Sew Step-By-Step

Introduction

Many people would love to sew, but they don't go beyond a few stitches with the needle and thread. However, everything changes when you have a sewing machine, because **you can do a lot of jobs in a very short time**. For this, learning to sew by machine is essential, something for which you have to have a little patience.

Parts of the sewing machine that we should know

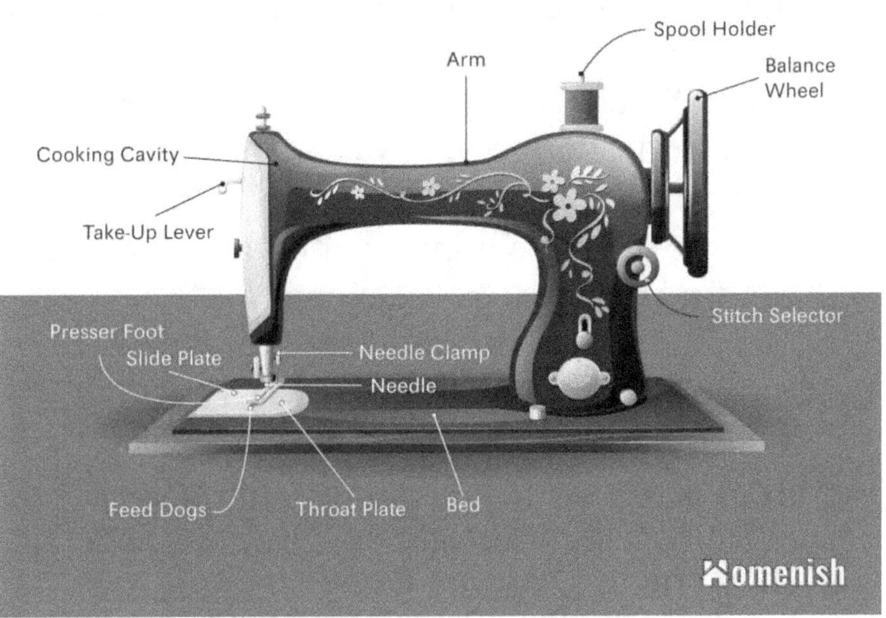

A sewing machine has a large number of elements:

- The roulette of the machine is the name given to a wheel that it has on one side. By turning it, it allows us to prick or remove the needle from the fabric. It is very useful when the needle gets stuck. Also, instead of using the pedal of the machine, you can start small by turning this wheel. It will go much slower, but it helps to learn little by little.

- The reverse lever is a small device that many modern sewing machines have. It can be said that it is the reverse button, so it is ideal for the seam finisher.

- At the top of the machine, we find the bobbin holders, where the thread goes. Depending on the thickness of the thread, we can adjust a small thread. As a general rule, they can be selected from 0 to 9, always depending on the thickness of the fabrics.

- Among the large number of buttons that we can find on a sewing machine, we find those to choose the width and length of the stitch. In each of them, we must select the appropriate number, depending on what we need. If we choose 0, we will make several stitches in the same place. The 1 is a very short stitch, suitable for buttonholes. The number 2 is for normal stitching and older serve to baste stitches.

- Electric sewing machines have a small drawer that can be removed. Here is the bobbin case, metal and easy to remove. We will only have to slide a front tab. Inside is the bobbin with its corresponding thread.

- The seam plate is the base where both the presser foot and the needle rest and is where what are known as feed dogs meet.

- The presser foot can be raised or lowered thanks to a lever at the rear of the machine. To be able to thread the needle, the presser foot must be raised.

Practice, the key to learning how to sew on a machine

After the theory always comes the practice, although we will not use cloth, but paper. It's a good way to avoid wasting fabric and learn to control the sensitivity of the machine's pedal. We can print different templates on paper that we can find on the Internet and prepare them for testing. We will turn on the machine and we will put the paper as if it were cloth. The objective is to follow the lines of the templates and do it with the machine without threading. It is normal that it takes a bit of work to follow all the lines, although in a short time we will master it.

The next step is to thread the machine, for this we will have to place the thread by passing it through the thread guide. Many of the newer electrical machines have drawings on it. Therefore, threading the needle will not be difficult for us.

Winding the bobbin is the next step, which consists of filling that bobbin with thread. In this way, knots and snags in the thread are avoided. To do this, we will remove the bobbin, then we will make a few turns with the thread and we will place it. When we step on the pedal, the winder will rotate and when the bobbin is full, we can stop stepping on it.

The basic stitches

When learning to machine sew for beginners, you start with the most basic stitches that can be given. In this case, the simplest stitch is known as straight or linear. It is ideal for taking our first steps with the sewing machine. To do this, we will only have to select it in the machine program. Then we will select the length we want for each of our stitch. Which should not be too short or long, we must find that there is a middle ground.

Another very simple stitch that is used by both beginners and people who already know how to sew well on the machine is the zigzag stitch. Thanks to it, fabrics can end up fraying. Therefore, after having sewn something or to make sure that this does not happen, we will select the zigzag stitch.

As with the straight or linear stitch, we can also choose the length that it should be, with which we will be able to reinforce the edge of the seam. Although we are learning to sew, we cannot forget a point of great importance that professional people also use, the blind hem. In this case, and as its name indicates, it is a kind of stitch that is not very noticeable. To achieve this, you must use a thread that is the same color as the fabric, or at least as similar as possible. In this way, we can reinforce the fabric without stitches made in another color and the work will look much better.

Now you can take your first stitches! Practice often and soon you will master the sewing machine.

Beginner's Sewing Guide

In prehistoric times, man sewed pieces from the leather of animals to be able to wear them on their bodies, this activity was done in a very primitive way but already there the art of sewing is appreciated and it is considered one of the first inventions of humanity destined to provide a comfortable lifestyle.

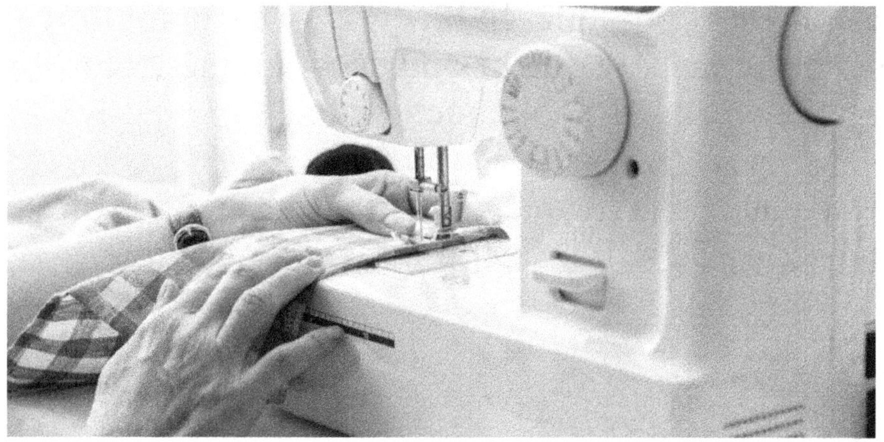

Sewing is based on the fact of joining two or more fabrics through threads and other materials, it is used to create clothes and items for the house such as curtains, bedding, upholstery and table linen.

Learning to sew pieces of clothing is a slightly more complex task because in this process the shape of the body, the size of the figure, the type of material and how to make it have a good drape must be taken into account.

Now, within the sewing process, different tools, materials and techniques are used that will depend on the type of piece we want to create and today we will talk.

It is common in many families today that there is someone who sews clothes for themselves and for the rest of the family, especially in the case of having to repair a piece that has a torn seam or that a button is missing; This is called "simple" sewing and on the other hand we have "ornamental" sewing, which consists of adding details to clothes in order to decorate, for example, with an embroidery or an application.

In the craft of sewing, the Industrial Revolution also played a very important role, both in the textile industry and in the clothing production machinery.

For this, the sewing machines that have evolved through history were created, in order to speed up the work and produce pieces in a massive way; An example to give us an idea: to make jeans you need more than five different sewing machines.

Sewing Patterns

A pattern is a template made of paper or cardboard that is used to transfer a certain design to the chosen fabric, to then sew and finally obtain a piece.

These sewing patterns are used to create clothing, dresses, accessories, cushions, and more.

They are classified into two main branches which are the domestic patterns and the industrial patterns.

DOMESTIC PATTERNS: are all those patterns made or worked at home; Among them we can find sewing patterns for beginners such as multi sizes or those that we make from measurements.

INDUSTRIAL PATTERNS: INDUSTRIAL patters are quite special for their realization since they are composed through a computer software or program called CAD (computer-aided design) or in Spanish, computer-aided design.

Sewing Classes and Tutorials

As we have talked about before, sewing is based on our liking it and taking time to learn.

We must turn to various sources of information to do a better job and become a specialist; such as sewing classes and tutorials.

These sources can be live or face-to-face classes or written or video tutorials.

Taking sewing classes is a good investment because in this way we can receive first-hand information from experts willing to listen to our doubts or explain us so that we understand the lesson.

On the other hand, the tutorials are an excellent way to learn new techniques and go practically at the same time that we follow the step by step.

Sewing Fabrics

Today there is an incredible diversity in the market of types of fabrics for sewing, colors and designs.

To get started, let's talk about its categories and how to choose the right fabric for our creation.

Fabrics for sewing are divided according to their structure and in a general way we can group them into 3 categories which are woven fabrics, knitted fabrics and non-woven fabrics.

- THE WOVEN FABRICS are of medium thickness, made by two sets of threads such as the warp and the weft and are very manageable as well as easy to work in the seam.

The sense of the direction of the threads is quite firm so to cut we must form 45 ° angles with the fabric.

Within this category we find sewing fabrics such as 100% cotton, torn cotton used in blouses, cotton canvas such as that used for children's clothing and underwear, denim to make jeans, skirts or jackets and others such as corduroy, gingham, calico and poplin.

Linen, silk, wool and microfiber fabrics stand out.

Linen is a natural fabric that is currently mixed with other fibers to modify its qualities and is woven lightly for blouses and heavier for pants.

Silk is a resistant natural fiber that does not resist the heat of the iron much; It is used for bridal gowns or blouses. Silk sewing fabrics include crepe, organza, and chiffon.

Microfiber fabrics are fabrics formed by nylon and polyester filaments, they are characterized by being light, durable and not resistant to the heat of the iron.

Wool is a natural fiber that is made pure or mixed with other fibers.

- KNITTED FABRICS are those that are formed by weaving meshes by interlacing threads and according to this they are classified into knitted fabrics by weft or warp where a different methodology and equipment is used to create them.

Weft knitting is a method of weaving a single thread from one side of the machine to the other under the needles to form a fabric that is then interwoven with itself to form a mesh.

This type of sewing fabrics are made up of basic ligaments and derived ligaments.

The basic ligaments of weft knitted fabrics are characterized by having a basic unit of the fabric that is the mesh as such and among them we find the jersey, rib, interlock and link-link.

On the other hand, the ligaments derived from weft knitting are those that contain the so-called loaded and floating meshes, among them the English point, Perlé and Piqué stand out.

- NONWOVEN FABRICS are one made of sheets of continuous filament fibers or chopped yarns, joined together by any means.

There are three main types of non-woven fabrics: disposable items, low-performance (or cheap) and high-performance, also called functional.

Among them are those that are created for medical uses, clothing and accessories, such as for the home that we detail below:

NON-WOVEN SEWING FABRICS FOR MEDICAL PURPOSES:

- Surgical uses: caps, gowns, masks, scrubs, and shoe covers.

- Bedding, curtains and hospital covers.

- Sterilization wraps (CSR wrap).

- Fixation tapes and wound care.

- Drug delivery patches.

NON-WOVEN SEWING FABRICS FOR APPAREL AND ACCESSORIES

- Interlining on fronts of coats, collars, lapels, among others.

- Disposable underwear.

- Part of the shoe as a buttonhole or shoelace reinforcement.

- Part of bags, wallets or briefcases.

- Bonding agent.

NONWOVEN SEWING FABRICS FOR THE HOME

- Abrasive sponges.

- Bedding, in spring cover and mattress top cover, padded backrest, duvet covers and pillowcases.

- Blinds and curtains.

- Base of rugs and rugs such as carpet tiles or bathroom rugs.

- Cleaning cloths for floors and furniture.

- Upholstery in inner lining, dust covers, padding padding.

- Table linen.

- Instant coffee and tea bags.

- Wall cladding.

Sewing for Beginners

At this point we can already realize that sewing for beginners is a bit confusing with both options and information to acquire.

So, let's take a moment to find out what we really need before starting on this adventure.

ABOUT THE TOOLS:

There are an extensive number of tools but it is important that we invest in some that are resistant to avoid breaking us in a short time and avoiding so much money.

You will need sewing tools to cut, measure, sew and other accessories that we will detail later.

ABOUT THE DESIGN:

We can also start using simple patterns (on the outside of the envelope you can see the level of difficulty) since these contain a reduced number of pieces and do not include the placement of buttons or closures.

At this point it is important that we check the pattern in detail to know what fabric we need and also read the instructions to know how to put our pieces together as well as other aspects of the design and if we want to customize it a bit.

Another important tip is that we have patience as care in the transfer of our pattern to the fabric, its cut and in the union of the pieces; It is a very important process and if we do it with difficulties as beginners, it is most likely that it will not turn out the way we want.

ABOUT SEWING THE PIECE:

We can do this process by hand but it is recommended with a sewing machine to make it simpler. Any sewing machine that works works well, as a beginner we do not need a very professional one but the one that does the basic stitches such as the straight, the zigzag and the reverse mechanism is more than enough.

About measurements:

When measuring, we must take into account two main ideas, the first is that the tape measure should not be tight to the body but with two fingers between it and the body; The second thing is that after taking the measures we write down a sheet and then rectify the measures taken.

Sewing Tools

For this activity we can help ourselves with various types of sewing tools, of which each one has a main function and that will make our lives easier.

For this we are going to divide them into sections according to the need we have at the time of sewing.

WHAT DO WE NEED TO MEASURE?

Before and during the manufacture of a piece we must be sure to take the correct measurements and bring those measurements as accurately as possible to the pattern or fabric.

This is where the importance of measurement tools such as the ruler, tape measure and all of those that we will talk about below is, because the success of our final result will depend on them.

WHAT DO WE NEED TO MARK?

Once we have the pattern with the correct measurements, we transfer it to our fabric to know where to cut and then proceed to sewing, but although it is true that we can do it by basting, there is nothing easier than using a pencil or chalk. to mark.

WHAT DO WE NEED TO CUT?

Surely before starting in the world of sewing, you did not imagine that there could be so many tools and less so many dedicated to cutting such as scissors, scissors, paper scissors, embroidery scissors, box cutter, rotary cutter and cutting board and the seam ripper...

TO SET?

To carry out fixing tasks we have different sewing tools such as pins, needles and plates.

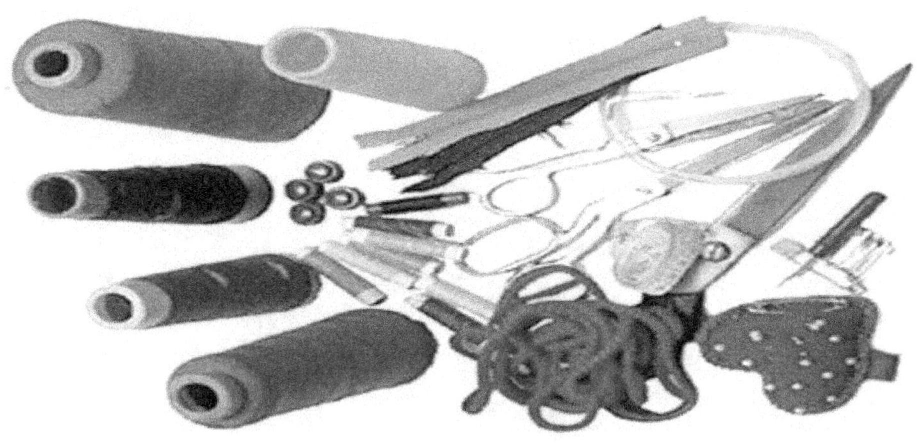

Sewing Material

Within these sewing materials that we mention, we will briefly explain the most used and their uses.

- Pattern: figure on paper of the piece to be made.

- Ruler: used to make precise traces of the pattern, includes a set of large square and a ruler for curves.

- Measuring tape: it is an easy-to-handle measuring tape because it is not rigid and has the numbering in millimeters and centimeters.

- Pencils: it can be in black and / or bicolor pencil, they must always be sharp to facilitate the work.

- Pins: used to fix patterns or join fabrics before sewing.

- Scissors: they must be sharp and are used to make the necessary cuts to assemble the piece. The scissors with which you cut the pattern paper should be different from the one you use to cut the fabric because cutting paper loses its edge.

- Needle: there are many sizes and thicknesses, it is used to join textile pieces.

- Thimble: hollow cylinder-shaped piece to protect your finger while hand sewing or embroidering.

- Notebook: it is used to write down organized data of the piece that is made, a notebook also works.

- Buttonhole open: used to open the buttonholes of garments such as pants or pockets.

- Sewing machine: it is the most useful tool if you want to create quality pieces.

Sewing Posts

Many of the topics that we are talking about here can be found in depth in our sewing category where we dedicate ourselves to talking in more detail and more precisely about each exposed point, as well as you can get ideas on how to create your garments and more.

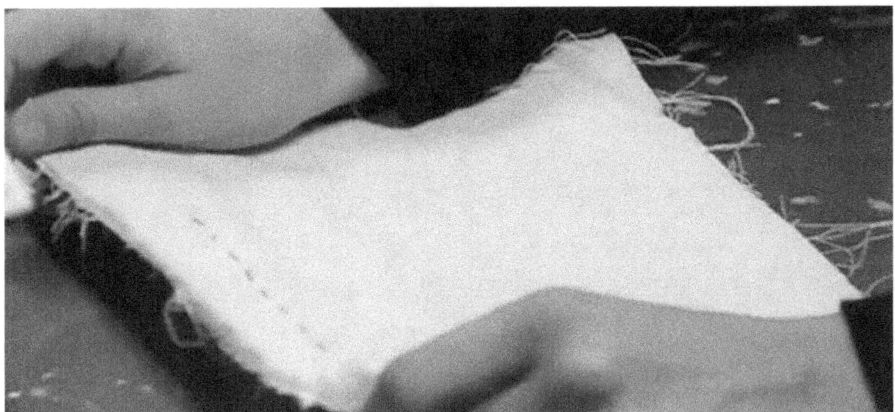

Sewing Techniques

Let's talk about basic sewing techniques, those that we need to know yes or yes before starting this work.

They are fairly simple sewing techniques that with practice we can master and remember.

OVERCASTING : this involves passing thread along the edge of the cut fabric to prevent it from fraying while we sew.

BASTING : before starting to pass the final seam, it is a good idea to baste, this consists of making a temporary long stitch seam; This is done in order to do a test, correct what is due and go to the actual final stitching.

FINISH OFF : once we finish the seam we must give two or three small stitches in the same place so that it does not come undone, this is to finish off.

INSERT THE hem: the hem is the hem of a trouser leg, for this you must measure, mark the measurement, fold, pin and baste and then sew the hem.

SEWING BUTTONS : in the market there is a great variety of styles and colors in buttons, we must ensure that the ones we use are in harmony with the piece we are creating. To choose them, take into account that the buttons come with two or four holes to insert them.

Hand Sewing

If we do not have a sewing machine, we must make use of **our manual skills** so we are going to talk about some of those stitches that we need to finish neat and without being overwhelmed by so much information.

Before starting the work, we must thread the thread, this is to place the thread in the water and there are two ways to do it.

The first is threading with simple thread that consists of inserting the thread into the needle and making a knot at each end, it is easy to undo in case of mistake and is used in embroidery for example.

The second way is double thread threading, which consists of inserting the thread into the needle and joining the two ends with a knot.

Now, let's talk about some stitches for hand sewing.

HEM stitch: It is the same basting stitch that we explained above, but it is also used to create gathers and prepare hems since it looks the same on both sides of the fabric, both from the right and the wrong side.

BACKSTITCH / BACKSTITCH : The backstitch or stitch is used to create a firm and resistant seam, it is used in those areas that are difficult to access such as corners. On the right side of the fabric, the stitching is displayed as a perfect straight stitch created with the sewing machine, but on the wrong side the stitches overlap each other.

BLIND HEM : this stitch is used to make the hems of the sleeves or waistbands, it is a BLIND stitch that is to say that it is not visible on the outside.

Sewing Machines

The own sewing machine was invented in the year 1790 by the British Thomas Saint that consisted of a manual machine that used an awl and only executed the chain stitch.

Then Maderspeger and Barthelemy Thimonnier built similar ones in 1830 but it was the latter's that was recognized worldwide since it was used to sew the uniforms of the French militia.

That same year, 1830, the first lockstitch sewing machine was invented in New York.

Later in the year 1850 Allen Benjamin contributed the rotary beret and four-stage intermittent feeding that advances the fabric between each stitch.

Currently, sewing machines play a great role in the textile industry, they have powerful motors capable of performing more than 7,000 stitches per minute. A breakthrough since its inception!

In the same way we can find sewing machines for special activities both for our homes and for large industrial productions; among them we find, for example, zig-zag sewing machines, making buttonholes, embroidery, sewing buttons, among others.

The sewing machine is composed of a fairly recognizable structure such as a base that supports the arm.

At the base are the mechanisms for dragging the fabric, on the arm are the mechanisms that make the movements of the needle and outside of this are the pulleys that allow us to tighten the threads.

Usually on the sewing machine it is possible to display the controls for stitch length, upper and lower thread tension and presser foot pressure as such.

Likewise, the sewing machine includes a mechanism for winding the lower thread that also serves to achieve good structure in everything we want to sew.

Let's talk about some types of sewing machines and their stitches:

STRAIGHT : it is a machine that provides only one type of stitch.

COLLARETAS : it is an industrial machine with which 3, 4 or 5 threads and 1 to 3 needles can be worked, this machine acts synchronously and provides a neat and attractive finish to the garment.

EMBROIDERY MACHINES : it is characterized by having multiple stitches and sewing patterns that add style to the garment.

OVERLOCK : with this machine we can make two types of stitches, such as the border stitch and the security stitch. It is used to finish clothes.

Now, another essential part for the whole process of sewing with the machine to take place is the needle itself.

Not just any type of needle is used for sewing and in fact they come in various presentations, but here we are going to study their physical characteristics in a general way.

The sewing machine needle should always be straight and sharp, if not, it should be replaced to maintain an excellent sewing pattern. The common sewing machine needle has the following parts:

HEEL : It is one of its ends that has a cylindrical shape and sometimes has a longitudinal section to better fix it on the grip of the lower part of the needle bar of the arm. We must make sure that it is well fastened before starting to sew.

CONE : It is the head of the heel in the shape of a truncated cone to facilitate its insertion into the needle bar.

TRUNK : in this part the truncated cone shape is maintained, it connects the upper end of the needle with the lower part.

SLOTS : This is a hole made in the length of the trunk in the front part of the eye for the shoulder and has the function of containing the upper thread during the passage through the fabric, in order not to cause friction. In some cases, it may be a groove on the back of the needle, but smaller.

EYE AND TIP : It is a small oval-shaped hole where the thread is placed. Below the eye is the tip, which must always be sharp.

Sewing Designs

The world of sewing is so vast that learning it requires dedication, but once mastered, you can create eye-catching and spectacular sewing designs.

Today we want to share some sewing designs that are our favorites and we love them.

For example, a jean with marked seams or a beautiful blanket made with the Patchwork technique.

Also, beautiful stitching designs for dresses that are versatile and for all tastes.

I would like you to tell me if you would dare to let your imagination run wild to create your own pieces?

Garment and Accessory Ideas to Enter the World of Sewing

After buying your sewing supplies and choosing your sewing machine, you will have to jump into action. But where do you start when you have barely mastered the sewing machine (**OVERLOCK**, fillet, buttonhole ...)?

"MACHIAVELLI (1469-1527) SAID "WHERE THE WILL IS GREAT, DIFFICULTIES DIMINISH."

However, when we start, it is better to start with easy things and opt for simple sewing patterns when reproducing them.

With will and work, you will be able to get there faster, but you do not need to exhaust the stages, since you will run the risk of falling into errors that are difficult to solve.

Before making an entire haute couture collection, you will have to **start with simple pieces, such** as cushion covers, pockets or trunks.

Here we leave you some sewing ideas from web 3.0, useful to give you creative ideas when it comes to putting your seamstress facet into practice.

Make a cake bag to enter the world of sewing

Here's a simple little accessory when it comes to making it: a bag for cakes and pastries. It is a cotton bag with cotton or suede fabric handles.

Thanks to the sewing tricks, I can transport my cakes in total comfort.

Transporting or keeping a QUICHE or a fruit cake in a cool place without the need for a refrigerator? With a cake bag it is possible. It's a great idea to go somewhere with friends or to make an original gift for Christmas, a birthday or Mother's Day ...

Next, you will find an excellent kitchen utensil.

What material do you need?

Two pieces of fabric measuring 45 cm x 85 cm to sew the body of the bag:
- A piece of cloth
- a liner
- a padding fabric

10 cm x 35 cm fabric to make the handles:
- two pieces of cloth
- two linings

Thermo-adhesive fabric

What procedure should you follow?

Fold the strips of fabric lengthwise and place them 1 cm from the edge along the entire length. Return to the starting point and iron the fabric.

At the ends of the piece of fabric, place and sew the handles, symmetrically about 8 centimeters apart from each other.
To keep the handles between the two fabrics, place the outer fabric and lining, right side up.

Fold each end of the rectangle towards the center and fasten. Sew the edges.

Once ready, what are you waiting for to start cooking cakes?

Beginner Sewing: Cushion Cover

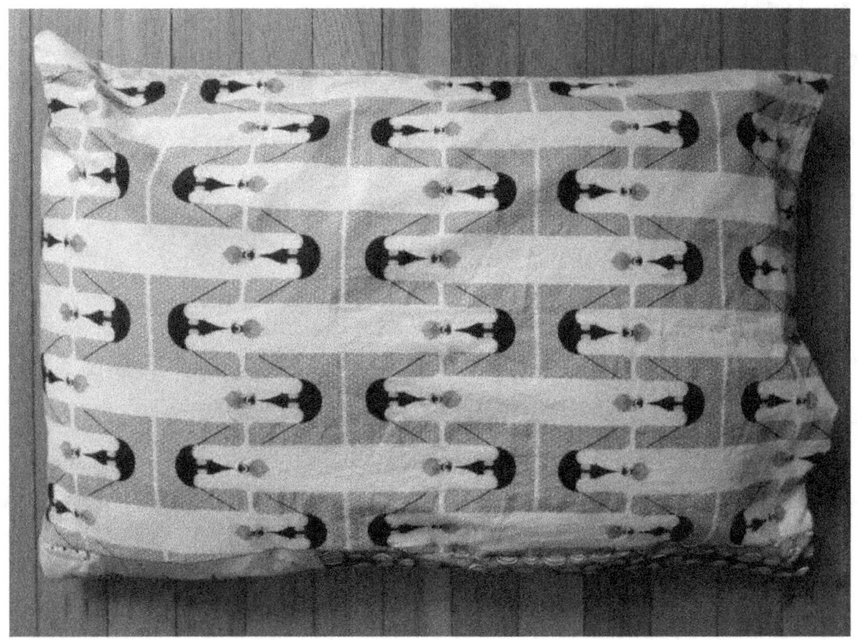

Why sew by hand when you can sew a cover with the sewing machine?

The cushion or pillow cover is the ideal exercise to learn to sew by machine, since we learn the basics: sew straight.

Material:
- Cotton fabric
  - Length: 2.5 x pillow length,

- Height: pillow height + 3cm,
- Thread.

Procedure:
- Place the fabric inside out,
- Make a 1.5 cm hem at one end with three fabric thicknesses (fold twice to "hide" the place where the fabric is cut),
- Place the pins,
- Sew the hem 1.3 cm from the edge of the fabric, with a straight stitch,
- Do the same with the other remote,
- Take a limb and fold it along the pillow,
- Fold the other end over the first so that the fabric is the length of the pillow,
- Put the pins from top to bottom,
- Cut top and bottom at the straight point, 1 cm from the edge,
- Sew the top and bottom in zigzag stitch to prevent the fabric from fraying,
- Turn the fabric over and you're done!

Now you just have to put a cushion and show off in front of your friends saying "I did it!"

Learn to sew: a handbag

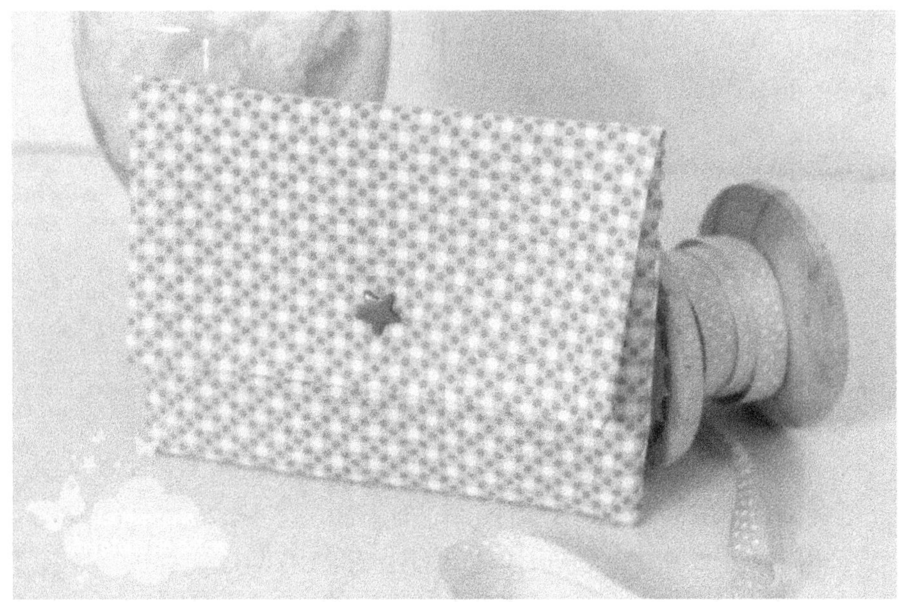

A little fabric is enough to make a bag.

Another good way to learn sewing is to **sew many bags**, of all colors and in all possible materials, to feel and learn to change the needle according to the thickness of the fabric, for example.

Material:
- Felt / Canvas 76 cm x 16.5 cm
- Headband
- Closing
- Thread

Procedure:
- Cut the fabric according to the pattern.
- Place right with right.

- Fold the wristband tape in half and place on one side, protruding and pinning it down.
- Fasten everything with pins.
- Sew in a U shape, the outside and the lining.
- Sew back on the part of the ribbon to secure it.
- For the cover, face the cover on the outside with the felt, align and secure with pins.
- Make a seam in the curved area.
- Once sewn, make a few notches with the scissors.
- Sew the cap part with the machine just to the edge with a seam.
- Once all the pieces are ready, assemble and sew.
- Fit the closure.

Easy! Once you have understood the principle, nothing prevents you from adapting the dimensions to make bigger, smaller, with or without interior separator, etc.

The bib collar for beginning seamstresses

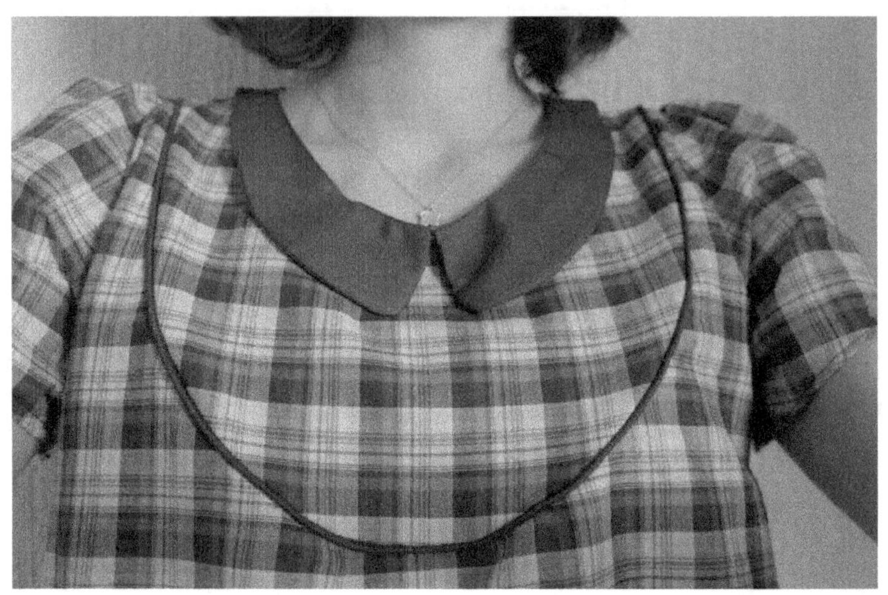

A bib collar that you can put on all your favorite tops, what a good idea!

The bib collar is in fashion and having one that you can superimpose on different garments is practical, don't you think?

It includes:
- 4 bib collar patterns in real size,
- The explanations step by step in photos,
- An explanatory page to use the thermoadhesive and its fabric well,
- A page with sewing tips and an explanation of the vocabulary used.

The 4 models use the same sewing technique. Then you can put a ribbon or a bracket to close it. Ideal for learning to sew straight, return to the right, mount and make a blind stitch.

Material:
- 30 cm of fabric,
- 1 clasp or 60 cm fine loop,
- Matching thread.

An easy-to-sew reversible bag

If you go to sewing classes, chances are your teacher will have you start with an easy-to-sew bag. On the web you can find free downloadable tutorials and patterns.

Material:
- Canvas fabric with world map print that you can buy at MC Textiles (1 meter will give to make several because it is double width)
- Matching gingham fabric
- Needle, thread, pins and scissors
- Pattern that you can download by clicking HERE . Print the five pages, tie them together with cellophane and cut out along the marked line.

Procedure:
- Cut 4 pieces of fabric with the pattern.

- We put the two main pieces right with right and sew the long strap and two with the gingham fabric.
- Layer both fabrics right to right, pin and machine sew.
- Sew the inner part the shape of the curve.
- Make notches (in a v-shape) all over the curved shape of the bag or use a scissors in the shape of a zigzag.
- Turn the bag to the right, take the fabric out through the long handle.
- Iron so that the seams sit well.
- Turn and join the short handle of the bag, join right to right, pin and machine sew 1 cm from the edge.
- Join each of the parts of the bag, right to right and leave an opening for the small handle.
- Pin, machine sew 1.5 cm from the edge.
- Backstitch 0.50 cm from the edge of the fabric.

Sewing a dress for beginners

A simple dress that you can make in different fabrics: lace, linen.

You don't need to go to online sewing classes to sew a trapeze dress, just by looking at some tutorials on the Internet you can make your own creation. Here we are going to explain what you need to make a trapeze dress for a girl. You can find the downloadable patterns on the web.

Materials:
- Half a meter in cotton, denim or poplin fabric,
- A back closure or buttons
- Half a meter of fabric for the lining
- 0.30 cm of fabric for the ruffles of the collar and cuffs

Procedure:

- We cut the different parts that make up the dress,
- We assemble the dress. Sides, shoulders and sleeves. We iron the rear sights and the hemline,
- We fold the printed cuffs strip in half lengthwise, close the ends and gather at the open part,
- We place it on the cuff starting and ending at the sleeve seam,
- Facing the lining and dress rights, sew along the views,
- And then the cleavage,
- The lining is cut the same as the dress, excluding views and 2 cm long,
- We put the sleeves inside the lining,
- To sew by machine, we put our hand between the lining and the dress until we reach the cuff,
- With the index finger and the thumb, we press the lining and the dress at the point where the seams of the sleeves coincide,
- We pull the two fabrics together,
- Without releasing them, we put a pin at that point,
- We sew the cuff by machine, joining the lining and the dress. The steering wheel is in the middle of both.

Sewing for beginners: boxes with recycled fabrics

This tutorial of home crafts teaches you in a very simple way to make a box with the recycled fabrics of your choice.

Materials for a 25 cm x 25 cm high box:
- Patchwork of fabrics,
- Scissor,
- Cloth glue.

Procedure:
- We will take the different pieces of fabric and cut five squares, four of these must be the same size, only one must be the same width but you must add a few more centimeters in length.
- Join all the squares with a sewing machine as shown in the image.

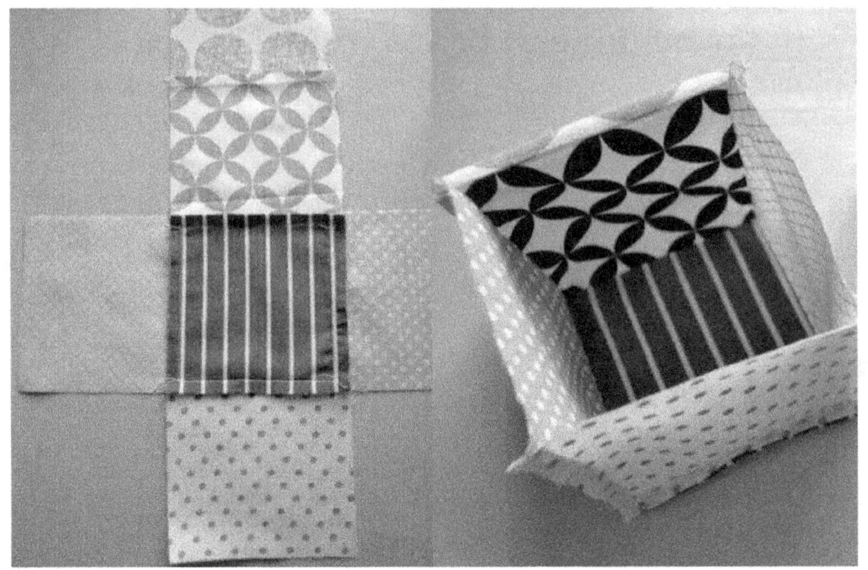

You'll see, fabric boxes are going to invade your home once you've started.

- Take fabric glue and start building a box by gluing the sides together.
- Lastly, take the fabric that forms the cover and stick a button on it.

Getting started in sewing: the folding bag that never wears out

This bag will be ideal for **learning to sew useful accessories** while reducing your environmental footprint. The collapsible cloth bag is a fantastic substitute for plastic bags.

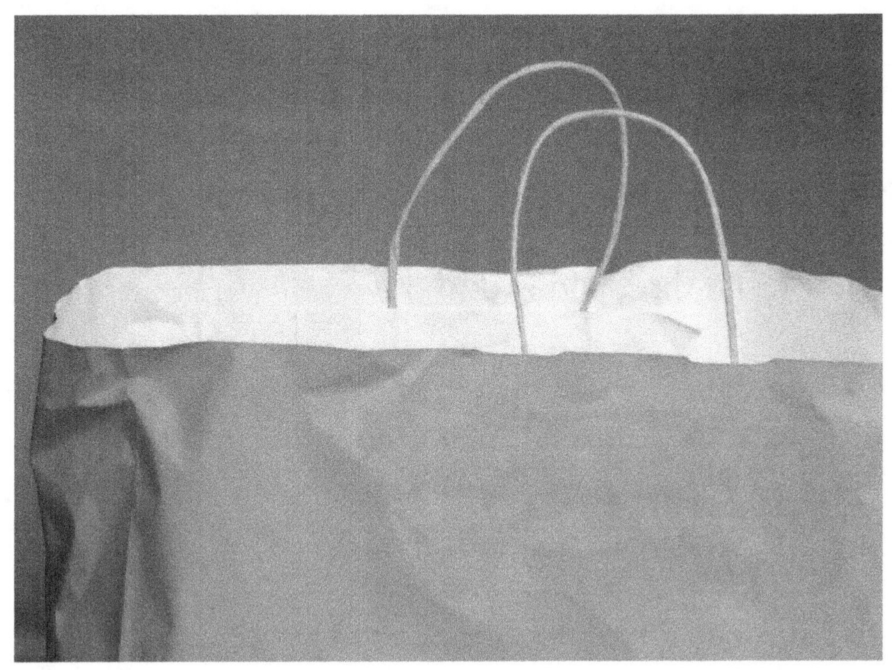

Of course, plastic or paper bags are much less practical and resistant than a cloth bag.

For example, you can use them to go shopping or to go on a picnic in the field.

What material do you need?
- A piece of fabric (organic fabric if it can be) of about 70 cm.
- 3.5 meters of tape.
- A brooch.

What procedure to follow?

- Cut the pattern fabric, then fold the top of the pocket - why? To sew the small side of the rectangles to be used as a storage pocket.
- Hold the two parts of the fabric (one close to the other and make a fillet, or zigzag stitch, on the three sides that have not yet been sewn.
- Then sew the handles of the bag 1 centimeter from the edge and iron, opening the seams.
- Place the tape on both sides of the bag, fold it over and stitch the edge 1mm to fix it on the fabric.
- Repeat for the handles.
- Sew from the handles to the bottom of the bag and then iron the pleats of the bag.
- Last procedure: sew the bottom of the bag 5 mm from the edge.
- Sewing tips and tricks: cotton blankets
- To make your own double gauze cotton blanket you will need a higher level of training but thanks to the online classes and sewing tutorials, it will not be an impossible mission.
- In case you mess up, you can always undo the mistake and make a patch.
- You will also need to know how to sew a button, join fabrics and upholster.

Thanks to my blanket, I can now sleep peacefully while camping.

Making a blanket is a bit more complex than making a bag, but what is better than making your own mattress for walks on the beach instead of buying it?

Here is the material you need:
- 1.20 m of double cotton gauze;
- 1.20 m of cotton double gauze of another color;
- 1.20 m thick wool;
- 2 kg of fiber padding;
- 20 buttons to cover;
- polyester yarn.

Manufacturing steps:

- Cut the fabric according to the dimensions of the sewing pattern, for example, into two pieces of 1.20 meters x 70 centimeters. Next, join the rectangles by gluing the outside side together as the outside side.
- Sew the sides 15 cm from the edge so that you can turn them around and place the padded side against the machine feet.
- Cut off the excess fabric with the scissors.
- Close the zipper, draw where you want to put the buttons on the blanket, and then sew them.

Know how to sew a purse

Here you will find a sewing blog that explains how to sew your own purse: the purse with a metal clasp.

Customizing your purse in various colors is better than buying a ready-made one.

The dimensions should be defined according to the good will of all, depending on whether coins, bills or cards are put in.

Here is an example of a 16 cm x 16 cm fabric purse.

What materials do you need?
- Two pieces of outer fabric measuring 16 cm x 16 cm.
- Two pieces of interior fabric of 16 cm x 16 cm.
- Four pieces of 16 cm x 16 cm thermo-adhesive fislin.
- A 9 cm wide metal clasp.

- An A4 sheet cut into small squares.
- A spool of thread.

What steps do you have to follow?
- Decide on the pattern you want to make on the four pieces of iron-on fislin.
- Copy the center line and the stripes will serve as marks at closing time.
- Glue the fislin pieces to the back of the fabric pieces.
- Sew the pieces of fabric from edge to edge, outside inwards.
- Hold the two outer pieces of fabric with the outer side facing in and lay them face-to-face.
- Sew the bottom of the purse 5mm from the edge according to the markings made on the lock.
- When you've sewn the outside, flip it over.
- Repeat the operation with the two lower pieces of fabric.
- Place the outside of the purse inside the liner (the two sides should be aligned, facing each other).
- Sew the top of the first half 5mm from the edge.
- Sew only half for the other piece of fabric.
- Flip it over and place the lining inside.
- Sew to close the purse.
- Sew the brooch by hand.

You already have your wallet ready to save money.

Do you want a case for your glasses?

Summer has already arrived and with it, the rays of the sun arrived. Does it usually take a while to find your glasses or do they get scratched when putting them in the glove compartment of the car?

"Customizing" or making a spectacle case is a good exercise in perfecting your sewing skills. If every sewing project has its set of difficulties, making your own glasses case couldn't be easier.

By reusing an old sewing kit, you can create your own glasses case or a toiletry bag to store your accessories.

What material do you need to make your case?
- 30 centimeters of cotton;
- 30 centimeters of thermoadhesive wadding;
- 1.1 meters of tape, size M;
- a push button.

What procedure should be followed to obtain a custom-made glasses case?
- Cut the fabric according to the pattern.
- Cut the iron on (in the direction of the glue).
- Glue the batting to the back of the fabric.
- Quilt the outside of the cover.
- Make a lining on the outside.
- Sew the ribbon onto the lining and place the pleats well.
- Lower the front and stitch 1mm from the edge.
- Close the cover by folding the top of the outer fabric.
- Attach the push button.

And ready. You already have your case ready.

Now you just have to store your sewing material in your basket or toiletry bag to replace your sewing kit.

The advantage of sewing is that it allows you to reuse those pieces of fabric that are no longer useful to make your own accessories useful in everyday life: hand-making may be a bit more limited for making clothes, but for bring small things and accessories, it is perfect.

In summary:
- Learning to sew quickly means **starting at the basics**, like learning a language, dancing or playing an instrument. Although it may seem repetitive at first, all learning requires **work and rigor.** It is the way to progress. You can complete it with classes.
- Sewing a pillowcase, a pouch or a reversible purse can be pleasant and you will also learn how to sew straight, use your sewing machine correctly, cut patterns or make a zigzag stitch.
- Before moving on to more complicated things, learn with simple things and **redecorate your house with boxes** or give a friend a beautiful handmade trapeze dress.

www.ingramcontent.com/pod-product-compliance
Lightning Source LLC
Chambersburg PA
CBHW060227170726
48004CB00004BA/1465